Advance Prais
A Hungry Soul Desperate to
Honest Prayers j

For a half century, I have directed people who wanted to know how to pray to the *Prayers* of a French monk named Michel Quoist. Now when they ask me, I will direct them also to *A Hungry Soul*, an exceptional collection of prayers by a Baptist pastor from Georgia named Charles Qualls. You will learn from both how to converse and commune with God in ordinary happenings of every day.

—E. Glenn Hinson
Senior Professor of Church History and Spirituality
Baptist Seminary of Kentucky

The readings in this book . . . are incredibly warm and sensitive, evidence that the author is a great listener, for he has tuned into our hearts with an uncanny, laserlike accuracy. He pays careful attention, the way a patient counselor does, and then speaks gently, as befits one who loves and cares. I cannot believe there is anyone whose life wouldn't be subtly and meaningfully enriched by spending an hour or two in the pages of *A Hungry Soul.*

—John Killinger
Author of *Hidden Mark, The Zacchaeus Solution,*
and *What the Blind Man Saw*

Sometimes we don't recognize our own hunger until we listen to kindred spirits describe theirs. In this gift of honest, sacred prayer Charles Qualls helps us hear our deep needs and God's abundant hope.

—Brett Younger
Associate Professor of Preaching
McAfee School of Theology

Smyth & Helwys Publishing, Inc.
6316 Peake Road
Macon, Georgia 31210-3960
1-800-747-3016
©2012 by Charles Qualls
All rights reserved.
Printed in the United States of America.

The paper used in this publication meets the minimum requirements of
American National Standard for Information Sciences—
Permanence of Paper for Printed Library Materials.
ANSI Z39.48–1984. (alk. paper)

Library of Congress Cataloging-in-Publication Data

Qualls, Charles.
A hungry soul desperate to taste God's grace : honest prayers for life / by Charles Qualls.
p. cm.
ISBN 978-1-57312-648-9 (alk. paper)
1. Prayer--Christianity. 2. Prayers. I. Title.
BV210.3.Q35 2013
242'.8--dc23

2012036799

*As always, Elizabeth,
you make my writing and
my ministry possible!*

Acknowledgments

• Dr. E. Glenn Hinson, who should not be held responsible for the shortcomings of my own spiritual development. But he did introduce me to centuries of devotional life and to the writings on prayer that reflected the wonderings of generations. I met him in a seminary classroom in fall 1988, and I have never been the same since.

• Mercer University, which provides a marvelous resource in its annual Preaching Consultation each fall at St. Simons Island, Georgia. The original inspiration for this book came from the 2011 meeting as presenter after presenter inspired me!

• The centuries of writers who have been brave enough to let us peek over their shoulders as they worked at prayer. That wonderful tradition of published prayer continues through today. The willingness to record what passed from their lips to God has given us a profound and humbling gift. This book is offered in that spirit.

Contents

Introduction

If we pay attention, life will parade before us an endless show of inspiration. Just as in comedy—where the best material writes itself—God's inspiration is without parallel. We are given better material for our hungering spirits than we could ever cook up from scratch. Sometimes our souls are more ready to receive this goodness than at others. And in certain seasons of life, we are more or less open to the meaning such inspiration can offer. We might see it in ways that help us to capture God's hope. The problem lies in figuring out where and how to use that vision. Life competes lustily with God's voice.

Part of how we *see* God is determined by how we *listen* to God. There is so much noise and movement in the world that competes with images of God. This noise would drown out God's beckoning voice and distract us. We might miss (and often do!) the *bath kol*, the ancient Hebrew understanding that God's voice is as soft as the cooing of a dove. We may not sense what spiritual directors love to refer to as the *thin place*—God come near. Have you ever allowed yourself to seek the safe space in the cleft of the rock where God passes nearby (Exod 33:22)? For along with the sacred and the profound come the fleeting and the foolish. How we filter these is up to us. But another part of how we find meaning is the movement of God. I believe that, if we are attuned, God speaks very noticeably.

I sat at the 2011 meeting of the Mercer University Preaching Consultation. If you have not been yet, I heartily recommend this annual event held at St. Simons Island, Georgia. Speakers such as Brett Younger, Tripp Martin, Colleen Burroughs, Tom Slater, Barry Howard, Rodger Murcheson, Carlton Allen, Dock Hollingsworth, and others stood in front of us. Each had from thirty to forty-five minutes to deliver a treatment of a ministry-related topic. Their work was inspiring, helpful, and—here is the important part—meaningful. In those sessions, they lay open their hearts and their collective souls. We laughed and even cried as we heard them labor at understanding this sacred work we share. I began to keep track of meaningful phrases from their messages. Sometimes it was just a word or themes that captured not only essential ministry but also important movements of God in our lives. Some of these tread on sacred and personal ground for me. Others compel me to reflect because they are urgent in the broader human spectrum.

Some of the phrases I jotted down that week form the titles for the prayers in this book. Other prayers you will read were inspired by reflections on life and spirit in the days after the conference. All of them give voice to what I hope is a part of your journey, too. These prayers are honest. They track my filtering of Emmanuel: *God with us.* They provide a window to my attempt to make meaning in life and to draw nearer to the mystery of God. My hope is that they will prompt your own voice of prayer. If this particular voice of prayer sounds familiar to you, then you may have read Michel Quoist's 1963 volume simply titled *Prayers* (trans. Agnes M. Forsyth and

Anne Marie de Commaille [New York: Sheed and Ward, 1963]). Dr. E. Glenn Hinson introduced me to that book, and the voice has been a part of me since.

John Killinger has defined prayer as "the act of being with God." We are often told by our church cultures that prayer has to have a certain language. We pick up and internalize phrasing and cadence that was handed to us from others who have attended our own churches. The saints of God have prayed in our public services of worship, modeling a fervency and formality (in many cases) that has stayed with us. Over the years, I have occasionally been turned down by a layperson when I tried to enlist him or her to lead prayer in a worship service. Most often, their plea is that they either "wouldn't be comfortable" or that they "don't know how."

I can't fix the "wouldn't be comfortable" part. But in the public or the private exercise of prayer, I hope I can be one voice in your life that helps you with the "don't know how." Prayer is not a formalized lingo. It is not an approved cadence or terminology. Killinger has it right. Prayer is simply the act of being with God. Some of it involves listening. We humans do not do this part nearly as well as we could. The rest is the vulnerability of speaking with God. Prayers in this book are uttered with words. Even so, many of our prayers seem to rise up from within us and are not as formal as even these simple verses.

Eventually, prayer is an expression of ourselves. We say something to God—somehow. How do you talk with those whom you know and love most intimately?

When I am at work or in front of a group, I confess that I weigh and measure my words carefully. Too carefully, no doubt. But the more I know and trust someone, and the more private our moment, the less formally I speak. How about you? With these friends or family, I loosen my emotional collar. I let down my proverbial hair. I am candid and natural. I think most of us are this way.

With our God, we are given unfettered access. And if we are listening to God's instruction, most of our genuine prayer is supposed to happen in the ultimate degree of privacy. No one is grading us on whether we prayed in King James English or in the language of our streets. The truth is that God is only grading us on our sincerity and our vulnerability, our honesty and our openness.

Preachers are sometimes guilty of living into a spiritual trap. We work in the Scriptures so regularly that we often view these productive moments as a substitute for spiritual discipline. Truly, we grow our faith in these moments as we write sermon texts or plan a study. But the prayers in this book came out of my exercise of responding devotionally to the themes I have collected. In a sense, my prayers have emerged through the keyboard and have been offered to God. In reading, you peek over my shoulder. In praying through these words—and considering the texts I have attached to each prayer—you join me in the journey. (Scripture texts are NRSV unless otherwise cited.)

As I live, I find that my soul is hungry. I am at times desperate to taste just a morsel of God's goodness and hope. I want to sample the grace that adds possibility and love to our living.

Be with God! You and you only. Within these pages, I am being with God—at least as well as I can, knowing that my church members might read these words, along with my mother. I have tried to forget those personal audiences for a time and to collect these prayers as unfiltered as possible. The texts that I have added to the end of each prayer are provided as a window to where my soul went in reaction to each. At times, you may connect in an obvious way with why that text spoke to me. At other times, you may simply be puzzled. That is part of the journey, isn't it? Perhaps I can add one more prayer to those that await you in this book. I pray that my effort here will somehow *release* the voice of your own prayer. If so, then my time in writing has been well spent. And maybe yours will be well spent in reading as well.

1

When a Word Is Spoken

"True love means never having to say you're sorry."

When those words were first spoken, what did their author have in mind? Because I have to confess, Lord, that I have never lived within the circles that would prove these particular words true. I have to say I am sorry to people all the time. This thought troubles me. And I think my prayer is shaped by what I have learned from that troubling.

Save us, O God, from a world that would believe such a thing. When a word is spoken, it becomes an undeniable part of history. I realize that I carry the power to bless—or harm—those I love the most. Only they permit me the access to be this close to them.

True, we can hope to exchange grace upon grace with those closest to us. In fact, those we love best may grant us the greatest mercy—mercy that rescues us with better than we deserve. This is a hallmark of closeness. Still, God, may we never grow so casual that we forget.

Forgetting will cause us to take for granted the need to create and recreate the gift of love. Love that reflects you. If we love, then we work at loving. If you have empowered us with the ability to become intimate parts of each other's lives, then you have also called us to bring quality and health to those lives.

Forgetting leads us to take for granted that there is room for healing. Yet we know the word [that goes?] too far, the thought that is too presumptuous. All of us have limitations, Lord. We all have that line across which we may step, only to be left for good.

True love means that we care enough to say that we are sorry when we need to. Help us to be willing to be this decent with our loved ones. And to try to catch ourselves before the egregious offense. For we know that grace is a gift, not a right. Mercy is a surprise, not an assumption.

When a word is spoken, it has been set free in the world. It is given life to create life or, in many cases, to wreak havoc in our relationships. —Brian Harbour, *Uniform Commentary,* September–January 2011, 2 October 2011 (Macon GA: Smyth and Helwys Publishing, 2011) 26.

If we put bits into the mouths of horses to make them obey us, we guide their whole bodies. Or look at ships: though they are so large that it takes strong winds to drive them, yet they are guided by a very small rudder wherever the will of the pilot directs. So also the tongue is a small member, yet it boasts of great exploits. How great a forest is set ablaze by a small fire! (James 3:3-5)

About Tomorrow

Tomorrow.

The word alone is enough to give pause, for wrapped in its syllables are promise and hope. There is the grace of time, too, which we will surely need now and then. I like the fact, Lord, that we get to start over and make a new one each day. A new tomorrow. There are times when I would like a near repeat of the previous day. But often I hope for better than I accomplished in the day just ended.

Tomorrow.

There is peril in this word, too. For so much mystery is found in it. We can account for the moment at hand, and we can only begin to explain the day that has passed. But tomorrow? How many tomorrows have brought surprises we could not have foreseen? Deep, profound disappointments. Happenings that threatened our very souls. And other tomorrows ended up delivering serendipities. Sovereign outcomes so wondrous that only you can appreciate their beauty more than we do.

Surprises, yes! Glorious ones that surpass the greatest anticipation of our dreams.

Help us, God, to make peace with the days that lie ahead. For tomorrow is a place we can only visit in our hearts. With everything that is rational, we know that for now we only see through a glass dimly. We must have your power in order to visit a time when that sight is crisp and clear. And when you do visit tomorrow with us, we view its reality through your perspective. Your wishes.

Tomorrow.

The future through my eyes might occasionally promise more than you intend! And tomorrow through my eyes will surely portray less than you hope. Give me the patience to traverse time's nuances only as I am in step with you.

Do not boast about tomorrow, for you do not know what a day may bring. (Proverbs 27:1)

So do not worry about tomorrow, for tomorrow will bring worries of its own. Today's trouble is enough for today. (Matthew 6:34)

3

A Prayer of Blessing for the Healing Hands

Our God, we pause just now to thank you for hands.

Not just any hands, though. The hands we need to be thankful for are healing hands.

At some point they became trained and prepared. Through the challenges of the classroom and the mentoring of the experienced, they were made ready for the job. We pray that those who use these hands will come to trust the background they were given long enough that they can become confident in their usefulness.

They are becoming skilled hands, Lord. So we ask your blessing upon them, for they must take the awkward tasks and make them natural. One moment requires sheer strength and persistence, while the next may call for the gentlest of dexterity . . . all to take expert care of those who are fragile and in need.

Help these hands to give soothing touch to patients who are fearful, and rightly so. These hands may be the closest contact they have to hope and promise of a better day. Lord, these hands will occasionally deliver a reassuring touch to those who love the patient. They will no doubt deliver a stern rebuke when firmness is called for. But in greater measure, they will lightly pat the arm of the worried spouse who keeps vigil and awaken the sleeping child.

These hands are available, Lord. For that we are thankful. There are other professions they could have chosen. But, before they learned to quiet the beeping machine or insert an IV port, they filled out the application to nursing school. Reward these hands with readiness, for we need them. We need them in abundance in our hospitals, our doctors' offices, and other settings of care. And not every task is glamorous. Reward their availability with satisfaction, O God.

Yes, we thank our Creator, who has made these hands. What they will accomplish, only time will tell. So much of what they do will be cloaked in the privacy of quiet rooms. So much of what they will do will be guarded in the confidentiality of the setting. But those who have been entrusted to their care will know what these hands have done. Appreciative family members, friends, and companions will know what these hands have given. Doctors and coworkers will see the quality of work that has been left behind.

And you will know—when no one else can—what these nurses have done. May you, O Lord, be pleased with the effort that has flowed from these servants. They have become ready. And so we commit them into *your* hands. As agents of your healing grace. As deliverers of your will. That all of humanity would live in the fullest measure of health possible.

We lift these prayers to you, the greatest Physician of all. In the name of Jesus Christ, Amen.

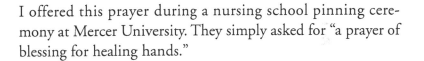

I offered this prayer during a nursing school pinning ceremony at Mercer University. They simply asked for "a prayer of blessing for healing hands."

The gifts he gave were that some would be apostles, some prophets, some evangelists, some pastors and teachers, to equip the saints for the work of ministry, for building up the body of Christ, until all of us come to the unity of the faith and of the knowledge of the Son of God, to maturity, to the measure of the full stature of Christ. (Ephesians 4:11-12)

Alone in a Crowd

A producer signals that she is "live," and her face enters literally a million households. Her every expression, wardrobe choice, and accuracy are evaluated by the opinionated consumers. Viewers comment on her makeup, her hair, and her weight too. She lives in front of the camera. People feel as though they know her better than they do.

The choir sings the last note, and then he strides to the podium. His choice of necktie is evaluated by opinionated consumers, as is his inspiration each week. He lives in front of the congregation. Sadly, they may applaud the brevity of his message more than the content of his words. People feel as though they know him better than they do.

The doctor commands a staff of support personnel, and her competency must be tested without fail. The teacher invests in students, and his wisdom must move the students forward consistently.

The counselor listens and guides, but who guides her? The officer patrols with alertness, but who protects him? The CEO leads with vision, but who leads her?

Oh, God. Do you know what it is like to be alone while sur-rounded by the crowd?

Hands to shake here, appearances to make there. People pulling, tugging, and demanding. Workers wanting validation, those who hurt seeking comfort. The sick and wounded beg-ging for relief. The press of availability can easily be mistaken for transparency.

Someone said, "It's lonely at the top." They surely tasted the isolation of responsibility. Those who know but cannot be fully known live in an odd marginalization. The friend accom-panies but secretly longs for a companion. The parent raises the child but desperately wishes for new love. Broken and spilled out, there seems to be no time to indulge the self.

But the lonely take other shapes, too. The worker at a large office who sits mostly invisible, somehow. The beloved daugh-ter who entertains at the family gathering but feels like the only single person in an otherwise married group. The fellow who walks the streets of the large city but who seems to know no one. The child who confides in a dog each day but is des-perate for human company.

God, are you sure you understand? So many turn to you each hour in prayer. You are never wanting for company. At every instant, someone is lifting her voice to you in thanks. In fact, we are reminded that humanity was created to be by your side.

You do stand at the door and knock, but far too few will answer. You know the nag of the presumptuous person who rubs at his prayer life like it's a genie's bottle. The hurried call for rescue reaches your ears more often than any other type of voice. Jesus listened to his closest followers and heard their misunderstanding. "My God, my God . . . why hast thou forsaken me?" These words were offered up by no less than the Christ of the Cross.

May we find comfort in remembering that you have known isolation. Though this should not be so, you have sensed the vacuum of the lonely space. For your love that surrounds us, we give thanks. For your life-giving presence, we offer our gratefulness. You are with each of us and near to all of us. That you have noticed us gives us hope, and that you respond to our cry lends light to our way.

Life gives us doses of both *loneliness* and *aloneness*. One of these can be painful and isolating. The other can be freeing and distilling. The challenge is to learn from the healthy alone times we have. This is when we learn about ourselves, and we can free our spirits to commune with God.

O Jerusalem, Jerusalem, you who kill the prophets and stone those sent to you, how often I have longed to gather your children together, as a hen gathers her chicks under her wings, but you were not willing. (Matthew 23:37)

The Impossible Call

He said I would have to make peace with it, this impossible call. And though I did not understand in that moment, I sensed he was right. For the call you place upon our lives is impossible.

The person who told me that? The one who pointed out the unattainable goal of your service? He did so out of the kind of resources we can only gather by living. That, and by the gift of your own ultimate wisdom.

Why have you placed such a burden on us, Lord? Why would you ask us to do work that you know we can't finish? When we love at our utmost capacity, there are more to be loved. When we give from beyond our storehouse of riches, there are still more who are in need. When there is no more time to share, there are more who need a moment.

The hospital is never empty, God. The heartbreak is never healed, the fears never assuaged. The lonely are never fully accompanied. The words are never exhausted, and the hungry are never fed.

Is this what Jesus lived with? Among all that He experienced on earth, please tell us that he knew the overwhelming sensation of the impossible call. You tell us that he has dealt with all that we will carry. Somehow, this helps.

So the load will never disappear. The job we are tasked with cannot be marked off the list. There will be more who need what we would give. Promise me, at least, that you will continue to call others. That you will take a few of today's hungry and turn them into tomorrow's providers. Tell me that you will carry those who limp into their service as healers. I want company, Lord. I want to feel that help is on the way.

Give me hope that others will put their shoulders to the impossible tasks of your kingdom. Meantime, I promise to keep trying. To get back up when I have gone down. To believe that you have a capacity built in to my ministry of which I have not yet found the limits. I will keep on because you have called. For now, that will be enough.

For you always have the poor with you, and you can show kindness to them whenever you wish; but you will not always have me. (Mark 14:7)

Then Jesus was led up by the Spirit into the wilderness to be tempted by the devil. He fasted forty days and forty nights, and afterwards he was famished. (Matthew 4:1-2)

Reeling in Rainbows

The picture made me laugh.

A rainbow hung in the sky, arched across the gray with all its mystery. With hope and promise, too. That much should not be funny. Wondrous maybe, but not funny.

No, the miracle of your love is sobering. However, the fellow at the photo's corner did make me laugh! Because the photographer set things up to appear as though this fisherman had the rainbow in his hand. Holding it by the bottom, he seemed to be reeling in the rainbow itself. The sheer entertainment on his face made evident a moment of joy.

No one was around as I saw the picture. Yet I laughed aloud at the image!

Then came the moment where I kept my gaze fixed on the picture. I tilted my head. For a time, God, I wondered what had caught my mind's eye. Something was so much more fascinating than funny. Then . . . there it was.

I want to do that. That thing he is doing in the photograph. I want to reel in a rainbow now and then.

We've all heard the explanations. Rainbows remind us of your creation promise. They change the skylines of our lives because they remind us that you have told us you would continue to work among us. That your gaze will fix on humanity for as long as time moves on. Your renewing hope for humanity presides where gray would otherwise prevail.

Help me figure out how to do what the photographer did, Lord. For that person looked at your Wonder in a different way. They tilted their head and used their eyes to see the creative possibilities most will not see.

I want to do that. With your help, I want to capture renewed hope . . . and for an instant hold it in my grasp.

May the God of hope fill you with all joy and peace in believing, so that you may abound in hope by the power of the Holy Spirit. (Romans 15:13)

By his great mercy he has given us a new birth into a living hope through the resurrection of Jesus Christ from the dead, and into an inheritance that is imperishable, undefiled, and unfading, kept in heaven for you, who are being protected by the power of God through faith for a salvation ready to be revealed in the last time. In this you rejoice, even if now for a little while you have had to suffer various trials, so that the genuineness of your faith—

being more precious than gold that, though perishable, is tested by fire—may be found to result in praise and glory and honor when Jesus Christ is revealed. (1 Peter 1:3-7)

7

I Know My Heart; Help Me to Know Yours

I know my own heart, Lord.

And it's not that bad a place. Inside it are locked the secrets I hold close. Thoughts that I filter for rightness and good. Wishes that might sound preposterous to some and inspiring to others. This heart helps me to stumble upon some of my best moments. Your direction of my heart brings victories that are pleasing.

Among its contents are some projects I may get around to one day. They would make my life, and the lives of others, better. These are the growing edges of who I am. They are guided by who you are helping me to become. I choose one of these projects now and then. Discoveries from this part of my heart freshen life with surprise.

Then there is the other stuff. Thoughts that even I am scared to admit reside there. At times, I think this content of my heart has its own space. I post a sentry to be sure no one gets in and to ensure that nothing comes out. The fact is, I am not sure I know completely what is in that part. I have an idea, though.

I know my own heart, Lord. At least mostly I do. What I need help with is knowing yours.

I, who guide others to know you, search to know your heart better than I do. I am desperate to know you better. I need to.

There are decisions that need to be made. Directions that need to be chosen. How can I build a house and plant crops on land I may not occupy much longer? My priorities of time and relationships need to be formed by your ways, not mine. My expenditures of money and energy need to be shaped by your hopes, not mine.

Is what I have given so much of my life to doing still what you would have me do in the days ahead?

I need to know your heart better. Suddenly, every moment I have let my mind wander as I worship feels wasted all the more. The days I have resisted the disciplines of spirit now lose some of their value. Forgive me, Lord, for the missed opportunities when I could have inched but a small amount closer to you.

Help me, God, to use the seasons I have ahead. Help me to learn—one awakening at a time—more of You.

Jesus said to him, "If you are able!—All things can be done for the one who believes." Immediately the father of the child cried out, "I believe; help my unbelief!" (Mark 9:23-24)

8

A Hungry Soul

I can live only my own life, Lord. The one that has been given me, and the one I have been given freedom to shape. On balance, this life is just fine, I suppose. Then again, I really have no choice about that. This life is the one I have. Wanting another accomplishes very little.

Of course, that does not stop us from trying to craft a different life. We dress as others dress, speak as others speak. We think after the thoughts of others and reach for the attainments we desire.

I am no different, Lord. Try though I may, I fall into the same patterns and test the same allures as most do. I am restless and fickle. I am greedy and cross.

In our better moments, I suppose we show you the potential you have built into us. We remind you of what you made us to be. In those brief seasons, we account for your image that is stored in each of us. In my best times I may even help you to smile. That's really what I long to do, I suppose. If it were possible to place a smile on the lips of God, that would be a worthy goal.

When I let myself stop—really reflect and gaze closely—I realize that I am a hungry soul, desperate to taste your grace.

Those words are scary to say aloud, even to think. For merely uttering them feels as though I am giving you more of the entrée. More chance to shape me. I love my control, and I love my freedom. Yet I also love the shadow of your presence. Your hand on my shoulder acts like a rudder that would guide. Your spirit's breath challenges me.

Famously, you meet me where I am. But you will not leave me here. I am more open to that shaping than maybe ever before. Still, I remain afraid of what you would do with me if I ever turned loose more of my control. Yes, I am hungry. Your grace accepts me beyond what I merit. Your mercy blesses me beyond explanation.

We know that we can hunger for what we should not consume. But this one pang is borne of your creation. This particular want makes no sense to me, but it answers a holy desire of yours. Visit my soul, Lord, that I may assuage a yearning that can only be sated by you.

At the 2011 Mercer Preaching Consultation, Brett Younger presented material under the title "Preaching to Would-be Disciples." Among the many compelling word pictures he offered came an observation: the people we would preach to are *hungry souls desperate to taste God's grace*. And when we consider that, aren't we all? Once I heard him utter these

words, I knew that I would have to write in order to more
fully process the riches coming my way.

*As a deer longs for flowing streams, so my soul longs for you,
O God. My soul thirsts for God, for the living God. When shall
I come and behold the face of God? My tears have been my food
day and night, while people say to me continually, "Where is your
God?" These things I remember, as I pour out my soul: how
I went with the throng, and led them in procession to the house of
God, with glad shouts and songs of thanksgiving, a multitude
keeping festival. Why are you cast down, O my soul, and why are
you disquieted within me? Hope in God; for I shall again praise
him, my help and my God.* (Psalm 42:1-6)

9
Inclusion

The target will not stop moving, Lord. How can we hit the center when we cannot get a fix on our aim? You see, a word of our time is "inclusion." We debate. We hate. We fight, we feud, and we fume. All around a set of differences that seems to change with each generation. With each century.

Why have humans struggled with the "others" we see? Gender . . . sexuality . . . belief . . . race . . . wealth. We will find something to square off about. From the safety of our distance, we stare. Ostensibly, we take comfort in being with those with whom we identify. It is easier to figure out what to talk about, what to do, how to act around those we think are like us.

We try to ignore the richness we miss as we exclude. We immunize ourselves to the hurt we might inflict through that narrowness. We distract our way through the loneliness we ourselves feel when it is our turn to be outside.

All are not alike, Lord. We must acknowledge that. When you made us, you did not use a form. You have allowed us to develop, to decide, as we would. We *are* other, God. There really are differences! We are other than you, to be certain. So we will go on noticing the differences. This much will not change, no matter what our hearts might wish.

Our God, help us with our issues of inclusion. Since the time you began uttering creation's words, you have had no such desire to exclude. All who choose to will indeed have a place in your kingdom. We may not know yet what to do with that knowledge. But it is true. May we be guided by your certainty, your love. We have been given the freedom to turn from you, but you do not choose to turn from us.

Thank you for the miracle of that kind of love, for its cleansing light dawns anew each day we rise up.

Blessed are you when men hate you, when they exclude you and insult you and reject your name as evil, because of the Son of Man. (Luke 6:22)

10

The Crush of Responsibility

"You're a worrier."

First it was a teacher. Then one family member and another. They told me this repeatedly. Okay. So I had a soul. At times, an old one.

Maybe I did worry too much for a kid. I wish I hadn't back then.

But now I have no such label. *Kid*, that is. I have moved on in life. My soul is still with me. And I care. At times, it feels as though heart and soul will collapse under the crush of responsibility.

Lord, I know we can care too much about things we have little or no control over. I know that we can add stress to life by misplacing our good will, or our fears, where we have little power.

But you made us to take some responsibility.

Because we have a soul, we care. Because we have a faith, we care. Because there is a Christ, we care. And the switch that turns care on and off disappears at times. I run my hand along the walls of my soul, but at times I cannot find the toggle. Help me know what deserves my worry. I am certain there are things that are worthy.

And form within me a better sense of those things that worry will not solve in the least!

Help me to trust, because you have shouldered the load since before the Word became flesh. We do not have to transport the payload of life alone.

Therefore I tell you, do not worry about your life, what you will eat or what you will drink, or about your body, what you will wear. Is not life more than food, and the body more than clothing? Look at the birds of the air; they neither sow nor reap nor gather into barns, and yet your heavenly Father feeds them. Are you not of more value than they? And can any of you by worrying add a single hour to your span of life? And why do you worry about clothing? Consider the lilies of the field, how they grow; they neither toil nor spin, yet I tell you, even Solomon in all his glory was not clothed like one of these. But if God so clothes the grass of the field, which is alive today and tomorrow is thrown into the oven, will he not much more clothe you—you of little faith? Therefore do not worry, saying, "What will we eat?" or "What will we drink?" or "What will we wear?" For it is the Gentiles who strive for all these things; and indeed your heavenly Father knows that you need all these things. But strive first for the kingdom of God

and his righteousness, and all these things will be given to you as well. So do not worry about tomorrow, for tomorrow will bring worries of its own. Today's trouble is enough for today. (Matthew 6:25-34)

11

Standing on the Outside Looking In

The cool kids really did look cool. I should know, Lord. I had a front-row seat to watch them when we were growing up. I wanted to be with them so badly. Wanted to be one of them.

At times, I tried. Too hard. That never worked.

Now I see them again. And a few say they don't remember me. That's because I was always standing on the outside looking in. But now some of them knock on my door. They hope I can help them find their way. Because they are trying too hard. Life has somehow left them out in ways that hurt deeply.

God, you watch us wherever we stand.

The thing I have noticed now, Lord, is that we are all just kids. Oh, we who are advancing are supposed to be seen as adults now. We qualify, if only by technicality. But even in the accumulating years of our lives, we are still experiencing so much for what seems like the first time.

You are the God of all the kids. In the chapters of life, you set the standard for what counts. You weigh the credence that is to be given, and your standards of what is *cool* hold steady.

Fear has grown up with us.

We make solutions to what perplexes us, trying to appear calm all the while. Thank you for the gift of perspective. Because at least there is context and, occasionally, wisdom. There is some measure of understanding. Hope, even.

If we have been looking at something other than the kids we think are cool—you have been there. Wanting all of us to believe that we are unique. That we are miracles of your grace, unrepeatable in design. You should know, Lord. Because you have a front-row seat to watch your creation.

For now we see in a mirror, dimly, but then we will see face to face. Now I know only in part; then I will know fully, even as I have been fully known. (1 Corinthians 13:12)

Finishing the Race We Have Been Given

This isn't it, God. I didn't sign up for this.

Oh, I have read the words. We are supposed to free ourselves of every weight that so easily holds us back. And run the race with endurance. At the finish is none other than Jesus Christ. The author and perfecter of our faith.

But this is not the race I wanted to run.

I had the route plotted out. My map made sense and was easily doable, God. There would be no inconvenience. No wrong turns. Only forward progress—and fast, too! I would enjoy the scenery and would know every twist and turn. None of them would surprise me. I would see them coming. My crowd—my people—would keep me going. They would be along the sides to cheer me on. I know this.

Because I planned out the whole race. So let me say it again: this is not the race I wanted to run.

Did I miss a meeting, Lord? How did this course come to be the one I would traverse?

I have noticed one thing about this race, though, Lord. The mileposts click by, each holding unexpected surprises. Things I could not have aspired to, you have placed along my journey. You have placed supporters along the way to cheer me on. Just as I have felt the dryness of thirst, life-giving water has been left by the wayside.

This way surely leads to an end. You know the map; its every contour and nuance is not a mystery to you. In fact, is that *you* I have seen along the way? A face in the crowd cheering; a hand to lift me up when I stumble? That person who mouthed an encouragement just loud enough for me to hear? That helped. These things sustain me on this race that I run.

That has been you, hasn't it, God? You have been there at points along the way. And you will await me at the end. The end . . . the finish of the race. The only thing you have asked of us is to finish the race we have been given.

The one we are actually running, but not necessarily the one of our choosing.

Therefore, since we are surrounded by so great a cloud of witnesses, let us also lay aside every weight and the sin that clings so closely, and let us run with perseverance the race that is set before us, looking to Jesus the pioneer and perfecter of our faith, who for the

sake of the joy that was set before him endured the cross, disregarding its shame, and has taken his seat at the right hand of the throne of God. (Hebrews 12:1-2)

Who Is Jesus?

Some assume they know. Some really don't care. Still others will not even permit the question to be asked for fear that wondering will take them too far.

Who is Jesus?

Is Jesus the one formed by the childhood drawings we saw? The ones the Bible teacher flashed up in front of us with his welcoming face? He held children on his knee. Small lambs, too, with his shepherd's crook raised in comfort. Jesus knocked at a door without a latch, waiting for us to let him in. The Christ of these drawings looks a little like me—and a lot like I want him to look.

We have seen images of a crucified Jesus, too. I need to see that one. But few have captured the sadness and rejection. Only the physical pain. We don't like that Jesus, because he doesn't make us feel "neat" or "awesome."

If these images formed my own picture, then what else have I missed? How is my picture somehow incomplete? What kind of Jesus did no one draw a picture of? My spirit yields over to these other artists. I let them form my own view.

I have not seen the picture of him leaning in the temple courtyard of my soul. But I know he does. Jesus stops by and props up against a column. Watching my endeavors of commerce and trade. Noticing as I tilt things in my favor.

There seems to be no picture of him retreating away from the masses. Worn from being pulled at and jostled. Trying to steal away from his world for a respite. I have never seen that one.

And now that I think of it, no one ever showed me the expression he wore as he addressed a brood of vipers. What expression did his face bear? As he grieved his friend Lazarus, few if any artists seemed to be around.

We mostly get the pleasant Jesus, it seems. The one who makes us feel good. The one who presents few challenges and who does not trouble us with his grief.

With this limited view, with these biased images, I realize I don't know Jesus that well at all.

I am the light of the world. I am the bread of life.
I am the gate. I am the Good Shepherd.
I am the resurrection and the life. I am the way, the truth and the life.
I am the vine; you are the branches. (from the Gospel of John)

14

Would Jesus Get the Job?

I'm not sure you would get hired, Jesus.

The fact is, you walked among us once and we did not recognize you. What makes us think we would know you if you did so again? Humanity struggles to recognize your presence, and the closer you come to us the more frightening and off-putting we find you.

Churches search for pastors to serve them. They bring in consultants to lead evaluation and visioning. They have conversations and hold big meetings. Surveys are completed and returned. Data is scrutinized and analyzed. Candidates read profiles to decide whether to put their names forward for consideration.

All of this honestly leads me to wonder: would Jesus get the job?

Everyone has her picture of what a minister should be. The one they would follow has held office elsewhere. They hope to find this pastor and steal him from some other poor church who would like to keep their pastor. They invite the prettiest and loudest. The largest personas and the best connected. They shape their searches with the best of their control and projections.

Meanwhile, Jesus steals into the room and does not bring with him either noticeable ego or large demands. Jesus' habit of entering into their lives on his own sense of time is annoying to some and weird to others. Probably not even an extrovert, he does not work the crowd enough to content some people. He does not shake hands vigorously enough, and one man says this stranger is not *dynamic.* One woman thinks this Jesus is too offbeat, too reserved to ever qualify as a candidate.

Jesus cares less about who gives what and more about the spirit in which they give. Jesus does not demand spotlights or use a smart board and dazzling show as he preaches. In fact, he sits while he teaches. His material seems a bit serious and rarely leaves his listeners feeling *neat.* Or *awesome.* That bothers those who want him to command the platform and put on a good show.

Some sense that if they choose him, Jesus will socialize with all the wrong people and draw the body into some of the wrong causes. Why, he may even take stances that seem foreign or wrong.

A few think he reminds them of someone they've seen before, but they can't quite put their fingers on whom. They think they'd better go with a more conventional candidate. No, I'm not sure Jesus would get the job. God, is there anything you can do to help us find the right one?

For in just a very little while, "He who is coming will come and will not delay." (Hebrews 10:37)

Behold, I am coming soon! Blessed is he who keeps the words of the prophecy in this book. (Revelation 22:7)

15

I Can Be Loved

I can be loved.

It's funny how some people don't even consider whether this is true of them. They may have struggles, but this doesn't happen to be one of them. They inherently feel loved. For others, though, this lovability thing is a tough hill to climb.

In Christ, you have loved me, God. Now I know. I can be loved.

I heard that I am supposed to love others as I love myself. But the mercy of Christ reminds me that on many days other people deserve better than that. Cognitively, I own that I am loved because my mind can make the case. My heart believes my mind better on some days than on others.

I can recall when someone has shared human community with me in ways that amazed me! Your people have made it abundantly clear: I can be loved. I have been loved by friends, by family, and by coworkers. My church members have made their love clear at times over the years. I have catalogued, somehow, many of these instances. The pictures dance through my head like an encouraging video.

Images of good times around tables, with laughter and good tales told! This is what love looks like. Visits on the front porch and the giggling of children. Travel with old friends, cautious outings with new friends. These have strengthened bonds and led to next times . . . and more. Congregants have sat in on classes and sermons, and have participated with patience. They have allowed me to call on them in hospital rooms and funeral parlors when they were hurting. We have held hands at the hospice, cried tears in the living room, and shared hope at the memorial service. These are loving acts in God's kingdom.

Forgiveness has been visited upon me, and second chances have been granted. This is love.

Neighbors have reached out with loving acts. They have come to our gatherings, and we have gone to theirs. Recipients of my own love and ministry express appreciation and include me in some of the moments of their lives that validate and bless. The file cabinet holds a generous sampling of written expressions that convince me of how surrounded by love I really am.

Still, sometimes I forget. Then I am reminded of the ultimate love of the Christ.

God among us has come that none would ever have to wonder again. I can be loved because Christ has already loved me! I can be loved, both by those who choose to love me and by the One who long ago came to redeem me. Thank you, God,

that you have embodied love in so many textures and sub-
tleties of life. We need every one of them in order to get by.

*This is how we know what love is: Jesus Christ laid down his life
for us. And we ought to lay down our lives for our brothers.*
(1 John 3:16)

16

Follow Me and I Will Make You Fish for People

Was that a promise you were making to us, Lord? Or was that something else?

I still remember the childhood craft project. We were in Vacation Bible School after my third grade year. I sat at a long table next to a window, and I was with some other children on the side facing the rest of the room. All around, we worked with the same materials. We were each given an oval bar of soap, a length of thin ribbon, a piece of fine mesh netting, and a small glue-on eye.

We were making a fish. The idea was to come away with a visual to support the Bible story for the day. Jesus walked along the water's edge, and he called some disciples. "Come. Follow me, and I will make you fish for people."

I heard your promise that day. And I still believe I should have.

For you were giving your word that they would be made ready for the task. Jesus did prepare them from that point on. Well, as much as he could. There were certain things that they were going to have to experience for themselves. And they needed the Holy Spirit breathed into them before they truly had the power!

I have taught and preached that promise. I have believed it for myself. My wife and I formed our marriage while talking of future dreams for life and ministry. Our life and ministry were born of that same promise.

But I have come to suspect that you were not just making a promise. "Come. Follow me, and I will make you fish for people."

I believe there was warning in those words, for I have found that there is danger in this fishing. Risk and investment, too. We leave behind pieces of ourselves as we venture out in Jesus' name. Those early followers eventually found out the same thing. They sacrificed themselves to follow this calling born by the sea. Deep prices have been paid for your kingdom, Lord.

So this promise is also a warning. What will we make of this duality in our faith? Each of us must decide. We must work out our faith. To this point, I am glad I did not know as an eight-year-old what I know now about that text. I could not have handled the truth, for you have been correct on both realities. You have provided in ways I could not see coming. And fishing for people has also had its costs. You knew what you were saying in that moment, Lord. I have been better for following the call, too.

In the childlikeness of my faith, I wonder what else I have heard in only one dimension.

Follow me, and I will make you fish for people. (Matthew 4:19)

Come to me, all you that are weary and are carrying heavy burdens, and I will give you rest. Take my yoke upon you, and learn from me; for I am gentle and humble in heart, and you will find rest for your souls. For my yoke is easy, and my burden is light. (Matthew 11:28-30)

The Perfect Church

We have all heard the joke, Lord. "Never join the perfect church; if you do you'll just mess it up."

But then again, this isn't much of an issue. Because we're not in danger of finding the perfect church to begin with. Help us to realize this, God. Right now, we grade our churches against a tough scale. We somehow expect perfection—or something that is so impossibly good that the church constantly fails. In comparison, she simply stands no chance.

The church has much against her record. She has not performed as you would have preferred. She has consistently taken her eye off the prize, the open fellowship of believers and community. The healing of hurts and equipping of saints can easily fall behind other concerns. Worship of you, rather than worship of the church herself, is always at issue. The church has chased after fast-moving, shiny objects.

The fact is, the Bride of Christ is limping along. Culture bears much of the blame, we could say. But that would only be part of the issue. Our confession would have to include our own distraction, distortion, and comfort. We would have to own up to exclusivity and pettiness at times.

Here is the rub: by definition the church must be flawed. For where you have called together your creation to worship, there will be imperfection. Humanity cannot bring anything that approaches your own standards.

We have tried, though. At least we have at times. You have guided us to do benevolent acts that few others would. You have given us a heart to show up when winds have blown, fires have raged, water has surged, and tragedies have struck. In our best times, the broken have taken sanctuary from their tortures among us. We have occasionally welcomed in the sinner, knowing deep down that they only join the sin we have already brought with us.

Help us, Lord, to move your church closer to what you want. We will miss the mark, but we must try. She will fall short. She will still disappoint. But you have ordained your church for the task. And she is the best thing we have.

Thank you, God, for the gift of the church.

I wish you would bear with me in a little foolishness. Do bear with me! I feel a divine jealousy for you, for I promised you in marriage to one husband, to present you as a chaste virgin to Christ. But I am afraid that as the serpent deceived Eve by its cunning, your thoughts will be led astray from a sincere and pure devotion to Christ. (2 Corinthians 11:1-3)

18

Unless You Come unto Me as These

This one is going to be a problem for us.

You know that most adults have forgotten that they were children once upon a time. In fact, how long has it been since most adults have included "once upon a time" in any sentence?

We get busy. We work hard to try to impress. Our images and attainments, our wants and frustrations become the controlling impulses of our days. And the competition. Lord, surely you have not known what it was to live in this literal and modern human race!

We project to each other some calculated persona. We niche our lives and focus our life energies toward holding on to that place—unless we spot another space that would suit our purposes even better. How much of ourselves do we give to trying to be grown up and polished?

Somewhere along the way, many of us lost vital parts of ourselves. We ceased to know even our own hearts. You beckoned us to turn around and come back. We heard your voice, but turning around was not in our plans. Advance, advance!

All of which makes experiencing your kingdom a difficult quest.

You have told us what this would take. That unless we approach you as a child, we would not enter into your kingdom. Yes, Lord. That one is going to be a problem. We hang our heads and walk away from that call. Because we know we have long since left behind almost every trace of our own child-likeness.

Those qualities of trust and goodness are difficult to access. Children express them so much better than we do. The abilities to give, to share, and to reach out in love? Little ones are so much better at that because no one has taught them not to yet. No one has lectured them on risk. Or attainment. Or position. Or "self."

Call out to us one more time. Call and keep waiting a little longer. In the meantime, may we see examples of childlikeness in others. May we value the qualities that are best accessed by being made a little lower than the angels. May we find a way to reconnect with the child in us—and with your kingdom's bounty of eternal hope.

Then little children were being brought to him in order that he might lay his hands on them and pray. The disciples spoke sternly to those who brought them; but Jesus said, "Let the little children come to me, and do not stop them; for it is to such as these that the kingdom of heaven belongs." And he laid his hands on them and went on his way. (Matthew 19:13-15)

19

Exhilaration Gives Way to the Routine

We live on the highs, don't we, Lord? At least you may have noticed that we try. Of course, this isn't realistic. But that never keeps us from striving.

We become accustomed to the thrill. Addicted to the high of achievement and feedback. We get used to accomplishment and growth. We craft our words and wait for hearers to smile when they hear them. We rehearse the song and listen for the applause. When the high note is hit, the reaction is noticeable. The peoples' appreciation is palpable.

In sports, we like the long ball! Homeruns, golf drives, 3-point shots and Hail Mary touchdowns—we like to see our athletes go for it!

But then exhilaration gives way to the routine.

On Monday, the adoring congregation has mostly disappeared. On Tuesday, the staff lines up to evaluate and inquire. The miles on the car document the hours spent alone. A chair is pushed up to the desk, where consideration and paperwork await. Planning, dreaming, wondering, and worrying. They come with the work, and they exact a cost.

We should expect this. After all, we cannot fly at such heights every day. Not every moment can find one a winner. For every sermon that can be preached, ten meetings must be had. For every soul that is transformed, countless others will not be reached. There are those who will make the church the center of their lives. But you know better than we do that more will come and go, merely consuming religious goods and services.

Help us, Lord. For in every line of work, in every family and friendship, we will not live only in the highs. There must be a routine in order for there to be a special occasion. We need your help, Lord, to appreciate the ordinary.

Yes, give us soul and heart. Teach us to see the gift of the daily and to find the holy in the mundane. That is where we live, really. We live so much more on the level plain than in the heights. And Christ said that this must be, for there is honorable work to be done. There must be a reason why life is as mixed as it is. We should listen to you and find out.

We need to ask for the ability to trust. You know what is best, and you know what lies ahead.

Peter said to Jesus, "Lord, it is good for us to be here. If you wish, I will put up three shelters—one for you, one for Moses and one

for Elijah." [5] *While he was still speaking, a bright cloud covered them, and a voice from the cloud said, "This is my Son, whom I love; with him I am well pleased. Listen to him!"* (Matthew 17:4-5, NIV)

Trying to Make the Unhappy Happy

Trying to make the unhappy happy.

There probably isn't much future in this, God. We like to be liked, and we love to be loved. At least some of us. Well-intentioned psychology has partly vilified some among us as *people pleasers.*

Take away any personal tendencies, and we are left with more practical concerns. The customer-service aspects of church prevail. We want people to be happy. We want them to attend in numbers that keep the doors open and the accounts full.

But we sense that service in your kingdom is not about saying "yes" to everyone who comes along. We can sell the store too cheaply, we realize. Some will mark one care off their list only to get upset about another. Eventually, we even suspect that much of their anguish has little if anything to do with you. Or us.

Some people are simply committed to being unhappy. Only you have the power they need.

In your church, it is not popular for people to concede this fact. They may not have even realized it yet. But they do not want to feel different. They have become used to their malaise. Their funk fits them well. Meanwhile, we keep trying. We expend personal, financial, and energy resources—goodwill, too. All in the cause of appeasing them.

Do I have a word that will thaw the heart grown pathologically cold?

Do I have an initiative that will charm them?

Do I have a story funny enough or a show entertaining enough?

Not likely. There may be no such thing, Lord, as trying to make the unhappy happy. And if we do, we may not be serving you as faithfully as we could.

When Jesus saw the crowds, he went up the mountain; and after he sat down, his disciples came to him. Then he began to speak, and taught them, saying:

　"Blessed are the poor in spirit, for theirs is the kingdom of heaven.

　"Blessed are those who mourn, for they will be comforted.

　"Blessed are the meek, for they will inherit the earth.

"Blessed are those who hunger and thirst for righteousness, for they will be filled.

"Blessed are the merciful, for they will receive mercy.

"Blessed are the pure in heart, for they will see God.

"Blessed are the peacemakers, for they will be called children of God.

"Blessed are those who are persecuted for righteousness' sake, for theirs is the kingdom of heaven.

"Blessed are you when people revile you and persecute you and utter all kinds of evil against you falsely on my account. Rejoice and be glad, for your reward is great in heaven, for in the same way they persecuted the prophets who were before you." (Matthew 5:1-12)

I Am the Way, the Truth, and the Life

Lord, we do not know where you are going. So, how can we know the way?

Beautiful words like these have helped my perception of Thomas move from "Doubting" to "Very Human." Thomas was willing to speak up and raise the question that others probably had, too.

If I had heard this back then, I certainly would have been as in the dark as they were. From the safety of millennia later, we feel compelled to act as though we understand what you meant, Lord. We carry a collected Bible around, some of us blinded by our comfort with its words. We lose touch with what we still do not comprehend, cheering for you out of loyalty more than understanding.

I am the Way, the Truth, and the Life.

This sounds good. It is the kind of phrase that would cause us to cheer you vigorously! We would stamp this promise on stickers, embroider this hope on pillows, and paint this challenge into framed art. Meanwhile, you have wanted these words written on our hearts instead. Then, we would spend the balance of our lives trying to live them out for you.

Help us to accept your permission to see you more as Thomas did. He was honest enough to confess that he still did not understand. Oh, the bold will witness of their absolute commitment. I pledge the same, and I toil at delivering my part of the bargain every day. We do not know where you are going, Lord. Not really. We know some of where you have been. We occasionally sense your presence as you are with us. But how do we get to where you are going?

I confess my ignorance. I will continue to strive to know you. I will keep working to sharpen my sense of your movement. Lead us, Lord. Help us to understand how coming to know you as the Way, Truth, and Life will help us know what you would have us do next. And in eternity.

"Do not let your hearts be troubled. Believe in God, believe also in me. In my Father's house there are many dwelling places. If it were not so, would I have told you that I go to prepare a place for you? And if I go and prepare a place for you, I will come again and will take you to myself, so that where I am, there you may be also. And you know the way to the place where I am going."

Thomas said to him, "Lord, we do not know where you are going. How can we know the way?" Jesus said to him, "I am the way, and the truth, and the life." (John 14:1-6)

Now—And Then—You Are There

A young mother holds her daughter in her arms. The toddler is crying because an uneven place in the sidewalk has tripped her. They are reminded that learning to walk truly is learning not to fall. The little one will not be consoled, because in that moment the pain and surprise are among the worst things she has yet experienced. Her sobbing grows loud and runs long. Her tiny perspective keeps her eyes from seeing how the horror of the moment will last only a short time. The mother scans the street to see if a face is visible on anyone's porch. No one is near, but she fears someone is listening.

Mother and daughter hold each other as the camera clicks away. This young bride is leaving her home. All grown now, she and her mother share a sisterhood. They can mutually confide, and they even advise one another. Over the years, they have entered into a collegial relationship. These two are friends. Their eyes see keenly a world that they can still conquer together. They need virtually no one, and they cherish their independence.

An aging daughter holds her mother and gives permission for Mom to die. Her frail body has become so limited. Ravaged by one disease, she cannot walk because she will fall. Her condition has been the object of pity for a while. Her eyes see little at all now, save a few shadows and shapes. She is completely dependent on her child for care. The daughter scans the hospital unit, confirming that they are surrounded yet somehow alone. Everyone has his own situation to tend. No one is near, but she hopes that at least a holy someone is listening.

Now—and then—you are there.

You watch all the activities of our lives. Your mysterious work in us is as ubiquitous as it is dependable. When we think that we do not need you, you are available still for those moments when we may wake up and reach out. When we know that we need you, you are closer yet. For all the ways in which you shape us, we thank you. And, in all the moments of your rescue, words fail to lend adequate praise for what you do.

Thank you, God, for you are with us both now and then.

For everything there is a season, and a time for every matter under heaven: a time to be born, and a time to die; a time to plant, and a time to pluck up what is planted; a time to kill, and a time to heal; a time to break down, and a time to build up; a

time to weep, and a time to laugh; a time to mourn, and a time to dance; a time to throw away stones, and a time to gather stones together; a time to embrace, and a time to refrain from embracing; a time to seek, and a time to lose; a time to keep, and a time to throw away; a time to tear, and a time to sew; a time to keep silence, and a time to speak; a time to love, and a time to hate; a time for war, and a time for peace. (Ecclesiastes 3:1-8)

23

Why Did You Call Me, Lord?

I have heard the "call" explained in every way imaginable.

Spiritual understandings are the rightful starting place. You speak a sacred claim on some of our lives, and we might hear. A few even respond. Handing over an extra measure of our independence in exchange for a lifetime of service is sobering.

A sociological view would hold that some surely find themselves distributed into helping roles within a world as vast and needy as ours. Just as some are craftsmen and cooks, doctors and dog trainers, others would give their time to service.

Likewise, our psychological friends view what we call ministry in most interesting terms. They will speak of unresolved issues, a need for being needed, and unrecognized urgencies that drive us. The voice of "call" is said to be a concoction directly from our internal world.

I ask only one thing: Why did you call me?

You could have asked anyone else to do this job. I have seen people who are more appealing than I am. There are speakers so gifted and minds so sharp that they would be worthy tools to pull out of your shed. There are quicker hearts and more patient souls. Some have creativity that makes me marvel. Others have insights I simply wish to borrow for even a moment.

Yet you called. And you place your calls on whom you wish. The fact is, we are all called by you. Every one of us has a path we are to follow under your guidance. All who pray could ask some version of this question, Lord. You have excluded none of us and have beckoned to all of us.

You have called me. I am just now entering into some understanding of both who I am and this burden with which you have entrusted me. I make peace with this call, and you show me more and more of it.

Let us continue this dialogue. You speak; I will keep trying my best to hear.

And I said: "Woe is me! I am lost, for I am a man of unclean lips, and I live among a people of unclean lips; yet my eyes have seen the King, the LORD of hosts!" Then one of the seraphs flew to me, holding a live coal that had been taken from the altar with a pair of tongs. The seraph touched my mouth with it and said: "Now that this has touched your lips, your guilt has departed and your

sin is blotted out." Then I heard the voice of the Lord saying, "Whom shall I send, and who will go for us?" And I said, "Here am I; send me!" (Isaiah 6:5-8)

24

I Tried to Say "Thanks"

Does it count as being thankful if I tried to say "thanks," but the person I was grateful to wasn't to be found? Does it count as being thankful if I tried to say "thanks," but the person I was grateful to seemed indifferent about my gratitude?

I tried to say "thanks." But I got no response.

Maybe the note wasn't ever received. Maybe the person thought the score was even, and there was no need to acknowledge my gratitude. Perhaps—and this one disturbs me—the person I am thanking really doesn't understand why I think they helped me. They might not consider the milepost I have passed to be a milepost at all!

I am learning, Lord, that my having an attitude of appreciation cannot always depend on getting the chance to speak my thanks. You have taught us to be thankful. Even more, you have taught us not to presume. A gracious spirit is not just a polite one. Feeling thanks in our hearts is an indicator that we are healthy in you!

People die before we realize what they did for us. We may miss the chance to thank them. People help us in one way, at one time, only for us to have the fruit of that help surface in some unrelated way at a different time. People have one set of values that cause them to invest in us. But their investment may manifest in something we do that they care not about at all! Still, they helped all the same. That much is not up for negotiation.

Yes, I think that we may sometimes try to express our gratitude only to find that we cannot.

Help me to continue to grasp that a spirit of appreciation is ultimately most important as a transaction between us—me and you! That will not preclude my still practicing the art and grace of telling others that I am thankful. But it will produce a healthier me that remembers that the best things did not originate inside my own mind or body. Instead, they were given to me by you.

Pray then in this way: Our Father in heaven, hallowed be your name. Your kingdom come. Your will be done, on earth as it is in heaven. Give us this day our daily bread. And forgive us our debts, as we also have forgiven our debtors. And do not bring us to the time of trial, but rescue us from the evil one. For if you forgive others their trespasses, your heavenly Father will also forgive you;

but if you do not forgive others, neither will your Father forgive your trespasses. (Matthew 6:9-15)

On the way to Jerusalem Jesus was going through the region between Samaria and Galilee. As he entered a village, ten lepers approached him. Keeping their distance, they called out, saying, "Jesus, Master, have mercy on us!" When he saw them, he said to them, "Go and show yourselves to the priests." And as they went, they were made clean. Then one of them, when he saw that he was healed, turned back, praising God with a loud voice. He prostrated himself at Jesus' feet and thanked him. And he was a Samaritan. Then Jesus asked, "Were not ten made clean? But the other nine, where are they? Was none of them found to return and give praise to God except this foreigner?" Then he said to him, "Get up and go on your way; your faith has made you well." (Luke 17:11-19)

We've Learned to Lust (But We Don't Know How to Love)

I settled into my seat, prepared to be inspired. My hope was that the speaker would teach me to do something. Help me to know how to use my voice better, tell funnier stories. Maybe use my audience's time more efficiently. That kind of thing.

Instead the speaker said, "We've learned to lust, but we don't know how to love."

And when I heard those words, I knew I was about to work rather than learn more about my work. Because now I needed to know why he said that. I needed to explore, God, how this observation was informed by life in your kingdom. Then, I allowed myself to listen to my own soul. Instinctively, I knew the speaker was right.

We live in a culture of expectation. We want things, so we buy them. No, we stalk things before we buy them. We tap our computer pads, and we switch our remote controls. We swipe our smart phones and surf the Internet. Change is literally at our fingertips. Attentions spans have shortened with all the quickness and variety.

Images of sex are as pervasive as our choices. We are surrounded by fast-moving pictures. The media is too easy a target, although it is certainly guilty of its own part. Yes, too easy a target because . . . that takes me off the hook, doesn't it?

Lord, forgive our shallowness. Our days are driven by incomplete fantasies that cannot satisfy. We do not invest if we cannot reasonably predict the outcomes. We do not stick around if the relationship requires effort. We spread our resources like fairy dust, but we do not really support anyone. We like our options open, our schedules flexible and our friendships casual.

We've learned to lust—but we truly don't know how to love.

Help us, O God, to cast our attention on the Christ. This One who showed us how to love. Who saw far past the initial glance, and who knew that our best qualities lie deep inside our personhood and not outside on our skin. Who knew that life was not lived in 140 characters and that meaning was not found at the checkout counter? Yes, help us to love more than we lust. Only then may we learn to do the things that matter.

Then the woman left her water jar and went back to the city. She said to the people, "Come and see a man who told me everything I have ever done! He cannot be the Messiah, can he?" (John 4:28-29)

Talk Less, Say More

What do our words sound like to your ears?

I wonder at times. We find Jesus' words a bit unsettling, especially that part about the "brood of vipers." That's some tough reading for us. We wonder if we are in that crowd, knowing instinctively the answer—that at times we are! But the inconsistency of humankind has to be tiresome to you.

We have invented a phrase: we call it *talking a good game* when someone fails to deliver. Others describe perpetual shortcomings as *all flash but no cash*. Either way, this has to be the light in which you see us when we fail you.

Preachers speak of the need to talk less but say more. As consumers of sermons, we might agree. The twenty-minute message has never been more in vogue. We now grade speakers on how brief they are, rarely concerning ourselves with whether we heard life-changing content. We talk about *economy of words* and the *craft* of writing that short sermon so that it will be most effective. *Be brief!* we demand.

But this is not just a preacher problem. For we could all stand to talk less and say more.

Surely you know my untruths before they finish leaving my mouth. The things on which I will not follow through. The oaths I take but do not mean. The intents of my heart that I am too scared to fight for.

Help me today, O God of my heart. Help me today to see the contributions my truth-telling could add to your kingdom. Please get my attention when a moment arrives to do some small thing that will reflect your greatest hopes. Convict me as an opportunity is about to slip by, and nudge me when I need to take a more positive direction.

That is all I ask. That I might talk less and yet end up saying far more.

Either make the tree good, and its fruit good; or make the tree bad, and its fruit bad; for the tree is known by its fruit. You brood of vipers! How can you speak good things, when you are evil? For out of the abundance of the heart the mouth speaks. The good person brings good things out of a good treasure, and the evil person brings evil things out of an evil treasure. I tell you, on the day of judgment you will have to give an account for every careless word you utter; for by your words you will be justified, and by your words you will be condemned. (Matthew 12:33-37)

Let no one deceive you with empty words, for because of these things the wrath of God comes on those who are disobedient.

Therefore do not be associated with them. For once you were darkness, but now in the Lord you are light. Live as children of light—for the fruit of the light is found in all that is good and right and true. (Ephesians 5:6-9)

27

If I Could Be Anything in the World

She was a child of God. These were the first words I spoke that day at the funeral. At the risk of sounding clichéd, I offered that this was the only time I ever actually led with that assessment.

There wasn't much else I knew to say. Her embattled mental state and her hermit lifestyle left me with few suitable words about her. Yet her family needed to hear something during the service. Before I told them of our church's ministry to her, before I tried to offer them hope, I simply reminded them that she had chosen to journey with you, God. This much I knew directly from her.

I have figured out what I want to be when I grow up.

If I could be anything in the world, the choices would be varied. When I was young, I knew that I would pitch in the

Major Leagues. There are times I might like to play golf well, and in front of large crowds. Other times, the life of a full-time writer might be fun. I tell you occasionally that I would make a wonderful philanthropist if only given the resources.

I would travel. I would help. I would learn to cook. I might even dabble in theater. I would do so many things if I could be anything in the world.

Alas, my course appears charted. My settings seem dialed in. With this reality, my soul appears to be at ease. I am none of those things, with little prospect of ever being them. Why am I content with this?

Despite the risk of again sounding like a cliché, I have settled into the notion that I want to be a child of God. In my best moments, I even act like one. This is easier said than done. If I could be anything in the world, that would be it. This much I know.

Well done, good and faithful servant! You have been faithful with a few things; I will put you in charge of many things. Come and share your master's happiness! (Matthew 25:21, NIV)

28
Slowly Making Our Way to Faith

My friends' snapshots were up on the New Members board. Mine was missing. That got me to thinking, and maybe it even gave the Spirit a chance to move. I began to ponder my own faith. I believed in God, and I believed in Jesus Christ. I had heard of my need to "accept" him. I told my mom I was thinking about making a "decision."

"Walk down the aisle, join the church, and we'll baptize you," the adults in the church said. "You'll be saved," they said. To this day, I still cherish my conversation with the pastor. I mustered the courage and made the long walk down the aisle. At least I could now take someone to the time and place where I accepted Christ.

Here is what the adults didn't tell me: in this lifetime, we are all slowly making our way to faith.

So comfortable have we grown with our church lingo that we make seismic decisions of faith sound like the flip of a light switch. My experience as a child may have been a significant milepost, Lord. But what I did not know then was that the journey of renewing and recommitting to my faith would be ongoing. This may be too big a transaction for any one moment in time.

Does that mean I doubt my salvation? Goodness, no. You know that between us, I feel like you are my God. You are the One who gets to decide whether I will someday make it home safely. I cannot do this. Only you have that power through Christ. Beyond that, though, you are constantly shaping me. You are constantly beckoning and teaching me. Your Holy Spirit visits upon me grace after grace. And the insights come my way in brilliantly dispensed doses.

This faith life is a lifelong journey that will not have a destination until you decide I have arrived. We have trouble admitting this, some of us. I resemble Jesus in one moment and bear only an image of a disheveled *me* in the next. You move me forward in one awakening, only for my development to halt there for a time. My doubts have been welcomed; my questions have only led to better questions.

This is the life, when we are slowly making our way to faith.

He answered them, "You faithless generation, how much longer must I be among you? How much longer must I put up with you? Bring him to me." And they brought the boy to him. When the spirit saw him, immediately it convulsed the boy, and he fell on the ground and rolled about, foaming at the mouth. Jesus asked

the father, "How long has this been happening to him?" And he said, "From childhood. It has often cast him into the fire and into the water, to destroy him; but if you are able to do anything, have pity on us and help us." Jesus said to him, "If you are able!—All things can be done for the one who believes." Immediately the father of the child cried out, "I believe; help my unbelief!" (Mark 9:19-24)

29
The Voice of God Like a Dove

If I listen, I believe I can hear you speaking. Why am I not more confident?

My native world is a loud one. Noise whirs around us in deafening volume. People talk, and machines do, too. Mindlessly, we turn on the television, the computer, the iPod and yearn to fill the background as much as we yearn for information. Come to think of it, most of us seek noise.

We have come to assume that you are loud, too, God. If we are more aware, we admit that we have fashioned an image of you after ourselves. Your voice of judgment is booming, but your voices of love and guidance are too. We like our preachers dynamic and our heroes charismatic! Deeds of ministry are hailed in large celebrations rather than in quiet closets of humility.

What is the price of this loudness?

The ancient Hebrews were onto something, Lord. They knew that your voice boomed far less often than it whispered. They called this subtle presence *bath kol,* a visiting by you that requires our listening. A more peaceful existence is needed, lest we miss your nearness.

You will call us. You will calm us. You will lead us. And you will redeem us. But in none of these cases are you likely to shout us down just to do so.

Help us to hear, Lord. Help us to remember to fashion more of a world that *allows* us to hear. As long as we fight to keep the volume up around us, we inadvertently stifle your voice. I have configured my spirit to assume that you will scream persistently.

All the while, I am vulnerable to missing your voice, which may reach out to me like the cooing of a dove.

. . . suddenly the heavens were opened to him and he saw the Spirit of God descending like a dove and alighting on him. And a voice from heaven said, "This is my Son, the Beloved, with whom I am well pleased." (Matthew 3:16b-17)

The Church We Don't Have

When we were young, we dreamed of a bigger church—one that was better known and that offered such diverse ministries that one could fit easily into the opportunities there. And a bigger budget would surely allow one to work almost without boundaries.

To serve with a famous pastor would be nice. To enjoy the renown that would come with being in our dream church. That would be good.

Then, later, the dream was to be part of a church that knew who it was. The diplomacy and confusion of multiple identities was stifling. Varying interpretations and labels, under one roof, felt like a millstone that held us back.

To serve within a congregation that had distilled its calling would be nice. To enjoy the freedom and clarity of a more defined setting seemed like a worthy dream.

And we have also dreamed of being in a place where people were more dedicated and faithful. Where one could know everyone's name. If we could design the perfect place, everyone would care about the church as much as we do. They would be uniformly generous and active.

To serve a body of believers who were willing both to think and to do—that would be nice, we thought!

Lord, these are our reflections when we fantasize about the church we don't have. Help us to mean it when we ask your help. When we seek your help with appreciating the church we do have, guide us to be satisfied. Not to be complacent and not to be blind about shortcomings. But instead to be appropriately thankful for the gifts all around us.

May you move us to focus less on our wish lists. Lead us to be about the work of building the church—indeed, the kingdom—that *you* don't have but are determined to bring about in due time.

I thank my God every time I remember you, constantly praying with joy in every one of my prayers for all of you, because of your sharing in the gospel from the first day until now. I am confident of this, that the one who began a good work among you will bring it to completion by the day of Jesus Christ. (Philippians 1:3-6)

The Good Gifts God Has Given

I am a person of expectation, God. A product of my culture, no doubt. But also impatient and a little demanding.

My computer cannot work fast enough, and my fellow Christians cannot be dedicated enough. My supposedly smart phone does not have enough features. The world around me cannot transform thoroughly enough, and humans cannot seem to be agreeable enough to please me.

And look at me. I am a mess. I am not as disciplined as I should be; I can be downright impulsive. I focus on things that do not matter at the expense of things that should. My work cannot be completed, by nature, for there is always another need to meet. Someone will always be begging for something, and I will never be released from my guilt.

Life is hard. We struggle, and we will not be released from struggle. Even when we should savor accomplishment or

peace, the memory of a shortcoming, a slight, or a disappoint-
ment flows in.

I have a tough time staying in touch with the good gifts that
you—my God—have given.

You have brought grace into my life. You have led others to
visit love upon me that does not make sense. Their inclusion
and generosity humbles me. You shower me with blessings—
specific blessings, were I to remember to gather them up by
name.

I have a sense of calling and purpose. There are victories that
you win in this realm, and we get to be a part of some of
them. There are second, third, fourth chances and beyond.
And the people. You entrust me with people to lead and nur-
ture. They do the same for me.

Today, in the stillness of the moment, I give thanks. For the
good gifts you have given, I am more grateful than mere words
will ever capture.

Blessed is a word that some use without considering it. So
steeped in the Christian lexicon, this word trips off our
tongues a little too comfortably. Then, there are others who
have overanalyzed themselves right out of speaking this word
at all. To them, *blessed* sounds trite, clichéd, or overused. My
rule of thumb is that if you know specifically *why* you say you
are blessed, then you are.

Blessed be the God and Father of our Lord Jesus Christ, who has blessed us in Christ with every spiritual blessing in the heavenly places, just as he chose us in Christ before the foundation of the world to be holy and blameless before him in love. He destined us for adoption as his children through Jesus Christ, according to the good pleasure of his will, to the praise of his glorious grace that he freely bestowed on us in the Beloved. (Ephesians 1:3-5)

A Voice Above Them All

32

He was not yet forty-five years old. A brilliant, tortured mind had been his to manage. Those who knew him said he had a lot of fun! They also said he had a lot of pain. No one could save him. He did not receive the help that so many wished for him. His death by his own hand broke countless hearts.

I felt so inadequate, Lord. The call was to lead them in a funeral. But the task was much greater. For there, my need was to speak on your behalf. And to facilitate another significant step in their grieving.

No words felt substantive enough. No matter how heartfelt my offerings, I questioned whether they would even come across as genuine enough for such a moment.

There we were. A portrait occupied a stand. An urn was featured among flowers. We prayed and shared Scripture. I spoke and offered them the best I had under your guidance. Variously, the organ played reflective interludes of comforting hymns. *Amazing grace, how sweet the sound . . . that saved a wretch like me . . . I once was lost but now am found . . . .*

That's when it happened. I could not see, Lord. But I could hear. That voice. Several among the gathering had chosen to sing along. I could hear the larger crowd casually joining in. Some of them mindless, others of them sentimental. Something, though, would not let go of my ear.

A voice above them all was singing with a different heart. Her words had a striking quality. Then, I recognized . . . his sister. She was the one I could hear the most. Some in her position would sing too strongly so that denial became their prop. Others would sing as though bargaining with you or trying to convince those around them that they were okay. None of these were her voice.

No, her singing sounded as though she was wrapping herself in the words. She was owning them with a steely hope. In that moment, I sensed that you had stepped through the veil. Your Spirit had known the way in. You were attending in ways that we could not plot or plan. Your hard work exceeded mine, and her voice served as notice of your presence.

I went there to minister, Lord. I wanted to give them my best. Instead, we all watched you come near. None of us can transform like you! Thanks be to the One who can.

For in hope we were saved. Now hope that is seen is not hope. For who hopes for what is seen? But if we hope for what we do not see, we wait for it with patience. Likewise the Spirit helps us in our weakness; for we do not know how to pray as we ought, but that very Spirit intercedes with sighs too deep for words. And God, who searches the heart, knows what is the mind of the Spirit, because the Spirit intercedes for the saints according to the will of God. (Romans 8:24-27)

33

Help Me to Be Grateful

We expect so much yet deserve so little.

I am a prolific consumer, Lord. In my home is enough space—and enough things—for a comfortable life. The fact is, double our little family could do fine here. Yet we find ourselves occasionally pondering what more of *this* or a larger *that* might be like.

We have people to make things for us here and people in other countries making things for us, too. Our appetite for possessions is insatiable. A simpler life might be nice, I *say*. A more cluttered life is necessary, I *live*.

But, Lord, my possessions are only a symptom of a greater need.

I have the gift of love in my life. People believe in me, often more than I believe in myself. Grace has rained down on me. This life I have lived is charmed by many counts.

Help me to be grateful. I know that a spirit of thanks, of gratitude, is something I am supposed to offer you. I am supposed to come to a stance of appreciation on my own. If I were close enough to you, I would be there. If I had enough discipline in my faith, I could not help being grateful. I am supposed to be grateful on my own, some would offer. This is a response you deserve.

Still, I have to believe that you can help us to move toward you. If we wait on me, by myself, I will give in to distractions. My gaze wanders; my heart wavers. Fill the empty places in me, that I would experience a richness and satisfaction only you can lend.

Yes, help me to be grateful. In noticeable forms and in the subtlest shades of mercy, show me the way to see the blessedness that touches me. For in thanks we move closer to essence of the Christ himself.

See that none of you repays evil for evil, but always seek to do good to one another and to all. Rejoice always, pray without ceasing, give thanks in all circumstances; for this is the will of God in Christ Jesus for you. Do not quench the Spirit. Do not despise the words of prophets, but test everything; hold fast to what is good; abstain from every form of evil. May the God of peace himself sanctify you entirely; and may your spirit and soul and body be kept sound and blameless at the coming of our Lord Jesus Christ. The one who calls you is faithful, and he will do this. (1 Thessalonians 5:15-24)

34

When We Preach

One more wind blows—just a small gust, really—and the right amount of force is exacted for a twig to fall. Actually, to *roll* is more like it. The twig tumbles the smallest amount forward and enters the water. From its creek-side perch, the tiny piece of wood had been a mere observer until now. All that flowed by was a show of sorts. Detached and somewhat irrelevant.

Ah, but that small gust.

Just the right prompting to cause a change for that little twig. Now the twig begins to move along in a branch that has flowed for centuries. Slowly at first, the twig becomes part of the drama. Just downstream, a mighty rapids awaits. Raging at times, the water has a power that contrasts with the stillness where the twig previously rested.

When we preach, we enter a stream of worship that has already begun to flow.

We should—therefore—have a good reason for doing so. When we preach, our worship has already begun. Fellowship has connected people. Songs have transported some hearts and souls. Symbols have set the mind free to contemplate. Rituals have reminded us that others have carried this faith before we did. Prayers have given word to yearnings, and perhaps lyrics have even voiced a question.

Now, the spoken word.

Lord, to some extent our egos allow us the boldness to climb into the pulpit. If we did not believe someone wanted to hear our sermons, we would not preach. We work at the craft; we hone our skills in order to be prepared. But may we humble ourselves before you when we preach. For even in offering a word that others would consume, we do so as participants in that worship stream.

Help us, Lord. Help us as much as you ever do. For when we preach we speak on your behalf far more than we do on our own.

If I proclaim the gospel, this gives me no ground for boasting, for an obligation is laid on me, and woe to me if I do not proclaim the gospel! For if I do this of my own will, I have a reward; but if not of my own will, I am entrusted with a commission. What then is my reward? Just this: that in my proclamation I may make the gospel free of charge, so as not to make full use of my rights in the gospel. (1 Corinthians 9:16-18)

35

We Wish to See Jesus

The image of Christ. Some would say we can never really turn this off. Oh, suppose we turn from God altogether. Then perhaps we can move away from being the image of Christ.

But others would argue that no matter how we act, we cannot be other than Christian—if our faith has been real to begin with, that is.

Some feel the pressure of living when so many watch. Both believers and those who have not embraced the faith watch those who have claimed the name of Christ. They keep score, these observers. They measure and label. They evaluate and talk. It never ends.

Faith is born of choice. It is sustained by choice as well. But faith carries obligation, too. There is a sense that once we put on the trappings of faith, there is a compulsion to continue wearing them. Care and feeding of the image can be

wearisome. Our Savior said that his yoke was easy and his
burden light. But his name lends weight that is at times difficult to tote.

There is fatigue to the faith for some. This much is unspeak-
able. This much is true.

There are always more who watch for more wholesome rea-
sons. They would weigh, measure, and evaluate. But theirs is a
curiosity born of possibility. For they watch to see if they
might like to take on this faith for themselves. On their behalf,
the request once was made: "We wish to see Jesus."

And so we continue to bear the weight. Our own souls are in
the balance, too. But others wish to see Jesus. The sermon of
our lives speaks loudest when we have no pulpit around. We
continue on, in part, to help you announce the kingdom's
reign.

Give us strength. Give us your grace. Give us the hope that
leads us forward to seasons where life in you feels light and
free.

*Now among those who went up to worship at the festival were
some Greeks. They came to Philip, who was from Bethsaida in
Galilee, and said to him, "Sir, we wish to see Jesus." Philip went
and told Andrew; then Andrew and Philip went and told Jesus.
Jesus answered them, "The hour has come for the Son of Man to
be glorified. Very truly, I tell you, unless a grain of wheat falls into
the earth and dies, it remains just a single grain; but if it dies,*

it bears much fruit. Those who love their life lose it, and those who hate their life in this world will keep it for eternal life. Whoever serves me must follow me, and where I am, there will my servant be also. Whoever serves me, the Father will honor." (John 12:20-26)

And He Passed Right through Them

Jesus went home and taught. It seems he was welcomed like a celebrity. Those who gathered to listen were proud. *He's so grown up now*, one said. *Can this be Mary and Joseph's little boy?* another wondered. *He must be successful; he has people following him around, you know,* one proud neighbor observed. *Yes, I heard he's even done a miracle or two!*

Then, he started teaching. The whispers continued.

Look how the young girls are watching him. He won't have any problem getting a date now.

I hear he has a book coming out soon! I'll bet his website is phenomenal. And the Twitter followers . . . my goodness. I'm so proud.

That's nothing—I dropped the words water *and* wine *into my search engine, and his was the first name that came up.*

I heard he was going to have to buy a huge auditorium because he's already out of space for worship. All those followers can't be wrong, you know!

Yes, and I wonder how long it will be before he has his own television ministry? Surely he'll go global with his ministry soon. Wait a minute. Did you hear what he just said?

Yeah, I was with him up until that last part. Seminary really messed him up. Made a liberal out of him!

How embarrassing. Insulting, even. How's that for gratitude?

Embarrassing—he can't say that . . . that's heresy! Somebody's got to stop this. Call security. Do we have security?

When this is over, his mother will never serve as president of our auxiliary again.

And he passed right through them.

When he came to Nazareth, where he had been brought up, he went to the synagogue on the sabbath day, as was his custom. He stood up to read, and the scroll of the prophet Isaiah was given to him. He unrolled the scroll and found the place where it was written: "The Spirit of the Lord is upon me, because he has anointed me to bring good news to the poor. He has sent me to proclaim release to the captives and recovery of sight to the blind, to let the oppressed go free, to proclaim the year of the Lord's favor." And he rolled up the scroll, gave it back to the attendant,

and sat down. The eyes of all in the synagogue were fixed on him. Then he began to say to them, "Today this scripture has been fulfilled in your hearing." All spoke well of him and were amazed at the gracious words that came from his mouth. They said, "Is not this Joseph's son?" He said to them, "Doubtless you will quote to me this proverb, 'Doctor, cure yourself!' And you will say, 'Do here also in your hometown the things that we have heard you did at Capernaum.'" And he said, "Truly I tell you, no prophet is accepted in the prophet's hometown. But the truth is, there were many widows in Israel in the time of Elijah, when the heaven was shut up three years and six months, and there was a severe famine over all the land; yet Elijah was sent to none of them except to a widow at Zarephath in Sidon. There were also many lepers in Israel in the time of the prophet Elisha, and none of them was cleansed except Naaman the Syrian." When they heard this, all in the synagogue were filled with rage. They got up, drove him out of the town, and led him to the brow of the hill on which their town was built, so that they might hurl him off the cliff. But he passed through the midst of them and went on his way. (John 4:16-30)

37

Wise as Serpents and Innocent as Doves

Lord, surely we missed something. After all, Jesus didn't give the disciples much to go on. His instructions were too simple.

In the church, we have built up the sharing of our faith into certification processes, study courses, and team-training modules. We have so complicated the work of the kingdom that no one feels qualified anymore. At least, many feel a barrier to doing something. Anything. Why didn't he give us more?

Instead, he paired them up and basically told them, "Be wise as serpents and innocent as doves." That's it! Well, that and to travel light and not hang around where they weren't welcome. This is what Jesus told them.

There's another problem, too. His words don't sound quite right. I have never seen a Christian store with these words on a throw pillow or a bumper sticker. They are neither warm nor fuzzy. Not awesome or uplifting. These words do not sell, Lord. They do not work for book titles, praise songs, or retreat themes.

"Be wise as serpents and innocent as doves." Really? Was that the best you had?

Then, we lived by these words.

Actually, they have aged well, Lord. This work is not easy. Loving is not always well received. You call us to be faithful but not stupid. Diligent but not irrelevant. Life calls on all the Spirit-led savvy and word-fed wisdom that we can muster.

Thank you for knowing what we need and when we need it. Help us to learn that loving is a tough choice at times. And that your work needs the same balance of intelligence and purity that all of life does.

These twelve Jesus sent out with the following instructions: "Go nowhere among the Gentiles, and enter no town of the Samaritans, but go rather to the lost sheep of the house of Israel. As you go, proclaim the good news, 'The kingdom of heaven has come near.' Cure the sick, raise the dead, cleanse the lepers, cast out demons. You received without payment; give without payment. Take no gold, or silver, or copper in your belts, no bag for your journey, or two tunics, or sandals, or a staff; for laborers

deserve their food. Whatever town or village you enter, find out who in it is worthy, and stay there until you leave. As you enter the house, greet it. If the house is worthy, let your peace come upon it; but if it is not worthy, let your peace return to you. If anyone will not welcome you or listen to your words, shake off the dust from your feet as you leave that house or town. Truly I tell you, it will be more tolerable for the land of Sodom and Gomorrah on the day of judgment than for that town. See, I am sending you out like sheep into the midst of wolves; so be wise as serpents and innocent as doves." (Matthew 10:5-16)

38

He Told Me Everything I Ever Did

The young adult fidgets in the chair, sharing details for the first time about his extramarital affair. The executive tells of the corporate misdeeds she has committed. A parent tells of a drug-addicted child and the warning signs he should have heeded. A grandparent speaks of determination to pitch in with the small children, then confesses that she never taught her own children much about making a healthy family. The veteran couple speaks of staying together for the children but also of their lost love in the marriage.

These are tough conversations.

Sooner or later, many of them turn toward *sin*. Yes, these people who recognize their own imperfections ponder how you feel, Lord. The fact is, a lot of them expect a spiritual whipping of some sort. They feel as though they deserve for the church to deal out some tough love.

And at times we must.

But we all have gone astray. We all have fallen short of the mark of your utmost calling. Given enough time, a frail humanity disappoints you, God. We disillusion each other, too. What can we offer to one another? What can help one who has fallen to get back up again?

A woman met you at a well. She had a conversation that turned honest at some point. Her sin was acknowledged; it was named unmistakably. But somehow she ended up repeating this confrontation as though it were the highlight of her life.

How does that happen?

It happens because, in the midst of naming a sin a sin, you gave her something else she needed: a fresh start. How could your simply talking with her do all of that? Some would miss the power in the conversation. Some would actually mistake it for judgment. She heard accurately, though. She picked up on the promise of a future, a second chance. Or was that a third chance? A fourth?

The grace of a new chapter is a gift. The hope that in our brokenness is new life. The reminder that now—today—is not the final word that can give energy to the lifeless! Grace to the sinner. Purpose to the listless. And perspective to those who have lost their way.

Thank you, God, for a time when you told a woman everything she ever did. For her story is our story. And the path to new life is paved with such love.

The woman said to him, "Sir, give me this water, so that I may never be thirsty or have to keep coming here to draw water." Jesus said to her, "Go, call your husband, and come back." The woman answered him, "I have no husband." Jesus said to her, "You are right in saying, 'I have no husband'; for you have had five husbands, and the one you have now is not your husband. What you have said is true!" The woman said to him, "Sir, I see that you are a prophet. Our ancestors worshiped on this mountain, but you say that the place where people must worship is in Jerusalem." Jesus said to her, "Woman, believe me, the hour is coming when you will worship the Father neither on this mountain nor in Jerusalem. You worship what you do not know; we worship what we know, for salvation is from the Jews. But the hour is coming, and is now here, when the true worshipers will worship the Father in spirit and truth, for the Father seeks such as these to worship him. God is spirit, and those who worship him must worship in spirit and truth." The woman said to him, "I know that Messiah is coming" (who is called Christ). "When he comes, he will proclaim all things to us." Jesus said to her, "I am he, the one who is speaking to you." Just then his disciples came. They were astonished that he was speaking with a woman, but no one said, "What do you want?" or, "Why are you speaking with her?" Then the woman left her water jar and went back to the city. She said to the people, "Come and see a man who told me everything I have ever done! He cannot be the Messiah, can he?" (John 4:15-29)

We Must Preach (Because the World Lies)

The speaker said, "We must preach because the world lies." And in that moment, I was reminded that one can both agree and disagree—all in the same split second. Everything our culture has told me cried out to say, "No, the 'world' doesn't lie. The world is simply a place of diversity!"

I even engaged the theological impulse to reflect that there really isn't a "World" versus a "Kingdom." All of the world exists within God's kingdom. All we see, I told myself, is of God's Creation force.

But in that instant, I also said—"You know, he's right."

From the earliest of time, it seems that God has yearned to have an alternative. An answer to the prevailing mindsets when they harm. God has worked to build a community that would challenge the most convenient and self-seeking ways. In moving among humanity, a consistent effort has been taken to provide a counter-action to injustices and excesses that rob us of our goodness. God has beckoned to gain our attention. And, to keep that focus which would stray to those things that entertain and pleasure us to distraction.

Our Lord, you do need us to preach! Because the World lies.

Who has the World lied to? David heard the blessing to kill so that he could gain yet another woman for his pleasure. Samson heard the allure of a woman, too, but her voice competed with his own needs for physical and intellectual superiority. Zaccheus heard that it was okay to take extra from those who would pay taxes because there was nothing they could do about it. James and John's own mother lied to them about what was important in Jesus' movement.

But, these ancient fibs were not the last. Today, politicians are told that brutalizing a clear path into office is the way we do things. Companies are told that shareholders are really, in the final analysis, all that matter. Churches believe that bigger and *hipper* is the only future. Adults are told that commitment to one partner is not possible anymore. And, they hear that impossible work hours are a valid way of parenting because the love behind lavish provision will be felt.

Oh, God. The World does lie. Uncountered, those lies become truth because they are repeated so often.

We must preach. You need every syllable we can offer and every challenge we can muster. Because you are love. And, we must hear that from someone. You are justice, and we must remember that. You are equality, and someday we must believe that. You are hope, and until eternity we will need that.

Give us voices that will not tire, souls which are nourished and hearts that are willing. Because, we must preach. The world lies.

They said, "What will we do with them? For it is obvious to all who live in Jerusalem that a notable sign has been done through them; we cannot deny it. But to keep it from spreading further among the people, let us warn them to speak no more to anyone in this name." So they called them and ordered them not to speak or teach at all in the name of Jesus. But Peter and John answered them, "Whether it is right in God's sight to listen to you rather than to God, you must judge; for we cannot keep from speaking about what we have seen and heard." (Acts 4: 16-20)

Standing on Broad Shoulders

We are standing on broad shoulders, Lord.

For all her imperfections, the Church has been crafted on wonderful and rich tradition that most of us cannot claim to have invented. Most of us sit on Sundays inside structures we did not build, and in seats we did not buy. We sing songs we did not write and listen to scripture texts we did not discover. Today's Church owes much to the men and women who founded her and passed her along.

We tweak a little here, innovate a little there. Some have even lit virtual dynamite and tucked a stick or two under her supports. They have rebuilt on forms and styles that seem fresh and new. Their song drives a different beat, their polity and priorities differ, too.

Some might even say that the Church today is nothing to be proud of. Still, she is the one we have! The Bride of Christ; an imperfect outpost on a frontier inhabited by imperfect persons, is now entrusted to our stewardship.

You know what? If someone isn't comfortable acknowledging the gift of the Church—we are STILL standing on broad shoulders in our beliefs.

This faith . . . there is no one alive who came close to inventing this faith we profess. We did not hear the Christ's bodily voice. We did not write down the teachings and we did not chronicle the earliest movement. Those words were preached and many hearts wrote them down. They were protected, these words, and a mighty Spirit's wind blew them through time. Struggle by struggle, and insight by insight, their mysteries have yielded riches. Centuries of courageous persons have ventured forth to tell what they believed. And, to confess their questions, too.

Quiet and loud, public and private, their musings have cascaded to us. A living faith.

Every bold pulpit, and every silent prayer, each missionary's zeal and every mother's whisper have carried your Hope forward. Lives have pushed the testimony toward us, bending time and trend to arrive to us today. The wonder of a faith that has stayed alive should cause us to marvel. The people before us did not have to entrust us with this precious gift.

Yet they did! So, let the eager student learn in humility. Let the tired veteran minister in gratitude. Let the layperson in the pew and the worship leader on the stage believe through the filters of meekness. For you have continued to press this faith forward. You have chosen to pass this faith along to us— and have gone to the trouble of handing it ever higher—until it finally reaches we who now perch precariously upon broad, broad shoulders indeed.

For we do not proclaim ourselves; we proclaim Jesus Christ as Lord and ourselves as your slaves for Jesus' sake. For it is the God who said, "Let light shine out of darkness," who has shone in our hearts to give the light of the knowledge of the glory of God in the face of Jesus Christ. But we have this treasure in clay jars, so that it may be made clear that this extraordinary power belongs to God and does not come from us. (2 Corinthians 4:5-7)

Made in the USA
Charleston, SC
17 December 2012